Aspergers CAN BE FUN!

Harrison and Charlie 7

HARRISON ALLAM

PARTRIDGE
A Penguin Random House Company

ISBN: Hardcover   978-1-4828-9374-8
             Softcover   978-1-4828-9373-1
             Ebook   978-1-4828-9375-5

To order additional copies of this book, contact
Toll Free 800 101 2657 (Singapore)
Toll Free 1 800 81 7340 (Malaysia)
orders.singapore@partridgepublishing.com
www.partridgepublishing.com/singapore

CONTENTS

Harrison 'up close and personal' with a sleeping koala at Albany W.A.

INTRODUCTION
ME, MYSELF AND MUM

Hi, my name is Harrison. I am 11 years old and had my official diagnosis of aspergers this year when I was still 10. My Mum and I have been working together as a team on my unofficial and official diagnosis of aspergers, and we believe we have a few strategies and ideas that can help you too have fun with aspergers.

We have written this book to help you in a simple way without too much theory, as we have found there are plenty of resources already available on that. Also, it is a very down to earth and very honest (in some areas too honest for me—as I find some parts very embarrassing!) perspective in a way that I hope you can relate to. Mum believes that my embarrassment may assist others—great!

Mum and I have been to workshops, read books, been to Therapists and have learnt a lot from all of them. We have also learnt a lot from each other and believe that we would now like to help as many people as possible in a variety of ways. We have come across those who are struggling with some of the little things that can sometimes be dealt with in a very simple way.

Mum and I also get to have a lot of laughs along the way, because it helps us to overcome the negative side that other people try to place on us or that can just happen, as life does.

Mum sometimes gets more flack than me. She has been told by her own family that it's because of her poor parenting for the way I am! When things are going good for us, she gets told that I must have a really mild case or that I don't have it at all. Now this really makes her mad, as Mum's basically with me 24/7 and they don't get to see what really happens.

As you may realise, aspergers is with you for life, you are born with it. That's no big deal because you can put things in place and be proactive to make it a real blessing in your life. Mum and I believe that we are learning all of the time, so we do our best to take what we have learnt and turn it into a great lifestyle for all of us. Sure we still have our challenges, but that's because we are still learning up until the day we pass on! What I have also learnt is that I'm not the only person going through this or feeling like this. Aspergers is 'real' and I don't have to feel ashamed. Each one of us who has aspergers or an ASD (Autism Spectrum Disorder) can feel our own type of 'normal' and there are plenty of us out there muddling our way through life, learning new strategies of how to make the best of it. Some of you will relate easily to what we have written and may have experienced a lot of it yourself, and in that, I'm sure we can also learn tips and ideas from you.

Where ever you may be on the spectrum or whether you have aspergers or not, I sincerely hope that you will enjoy our book and know that you are a special person with unique and wonderful abilities. We also hope to touch your sense of humour and give you a bit of a laugh with some of my own misfortunes and maybe learn some new strategies to help you on your own journey.

Harrison practicing "Pirates of the Caribbean" theme song on piano.

CHAPTER 1

THE KISS PRINCIPLE, KEEPING IT SIMPLE SILLY!

Where do we start? I thought we'd start with some easy things and then get into the more complicated areas as we continue on.

Daily routine! Mum is ex-Army and she can be go go go! So Mum can find it really frustrating when I am a lot slower than her in the mornings (or most times). It's not that I try to be slow, as Mum sometimes thinks—it's just that I seem to have to take my time with most things that she finds easy. It takes me awhile to get there.

To try not to drive Mum insane, we keep it pretty simple in the mornings. Mum usually gets my clothes out for me the night before and I know they are the ones I put on in the morning. If Mum forgets to do this and I grab my own clothes—guaranteed, I will grab the wrong ones—usually anything I first see—so they could be dirty or have holes in them, but I'm not bothered as long as they are comfy! I would live in tracky dacks if I could! And comfy t-shirts with no tag in them, as I find the tags scratchie. Mum has tried me in jeans and I can sometimes get away with cargo pants, but basically—I love comfy tracky dacks or comfy shorts that are similar to tracky dacks! I like the way they feel on my skin and they are not too tight. (Mum likes that they are heaps cheaper than jeans and cargo pants!)

Due to my balance and coordination I have had to wear orthotics since I was two years of age. I walked on my knees up until 19 months, and Mum says I was really fast—but I had flat knees and would wear holes in my clothes at the knees instead of in my shoes. Lucky I was able to get used to orthotics from that age, and I persevere now as I know they help me. But, if I could, I would wear crocs every day all day—again they are the most comfy. I have about 5 different pairs of crocs and one pair of decent walking shoes that I wear my orthotics in. So, my clothing is pretty easy and I'm happy to wear the same.

Breakfast is also pretty easy. I eat cereal most days and some days toasted muffins. I can now get the cereal myself. Pouring the milk in was tricky, but we use the one litre cartons. Mum puts the cereal in an easy pour plastic container and that helps. If I had my way, I would be happy to eat a sweet type of cereal each day, but Mum makes sure I eat something more nutritious. I used to eat weetbix with honey but got bored with that so now I eat a mixture of bland tropicos and honey rings. I won't touch muesli, cornflakes that taste like cardboard and anything that even looks like it has nuts in it.

Then really it's just teeth brushing time—and you think that would be the easiest! Not for me, apparently it's one of those sensory things.

Mum now takes me to the Dentist (a lovely man) who gives me a 'scale and clean' every 6 months. My Dentist still struggles to give me a full scale and clean, but he does make some progress in between my anxiety bursts. I also get a reward afterwards! Last time it was some lego. That sort of helped me to sit it out even though it was really really hard.

I have all types of toothbrushes to make it easier! I even have an electric one that helps some times. Mum used to tell me my teeth would fall out if I didn't take care of them. I was worried about that until the Dentist reassured me that I was going o'k with my cleaning. He did suggest that Mum still clean them for me at times when they are looking a bit discoloured. Mum and I really both dislike this, as it feels like Mum is pushing my teeth through to the back of my head. I have to hold on to the door or wall and try not to scream as she does it. She tries to be super quick!

Oh, shower time—I guess you're wondering if that should be part of my morning routine. Well, Mum tries! Especially if I have an accident—Mum says I smell, but I would rather opt for 'men's perfume' than a shower. When I was really little Mum used to say that if I didn't wash my willy properly that it would go black and fall off! I was horrified and as I take things literally, I believed her. It worked until I learnt it was one of those 'figures of speech' (only a few years ago!) and that it was important to keep clean, but that it wouldn't go black and fall off!

Washing my hair! Mum reckons all of the next door neighbours would think she was murdering me. I would hold the dry face washer over my eyes and Mum would be super quick with shampooing my hair. We still use baby shampoo that does not sting my eyes—well, I still reckon it stings! And there is no way I'm conditioning as well! Now I can try and do it myself, but sometimes Mum reckons I still have shampoo left in it because I don't rinse it well enough. I can live with that!

And I never brush my hair! This drives Mum a bit crazy and she books me in to our hairdresser whenever it starts looking too long. We are very lucky that my hair dresser is very understanding of sensory issues and people with special needs. Recently they phoned to say that I had to change my appointment and have it with someone else. Mum gave me two days to think about it, but I still said 'no' and was happy to wait until my usual hairdresser was available again. I can live with that too, not sure if Mum can though!

So, we've got dressed (after maybe having a shower and maybe washing my hair!) had breaky and brushed my teeth. I'm now ready to go! The best part is that if I stay on track with this routine I'm allowed to watch ABC3 on TV while having breaky—but if I start playing or become distracted the TV goes off! I would prefer to stay on track and have the TV on.

A few bonuses with hair and teeth sensory issues—The bonus about my hair sensory issue is that it saves a heap of money on shampoo, haircuts and you don't even have to own a hairbrush! And with my teeth, getting a reward for a scale and clean is a great bonus, considering it is very traumatic for me.

When I was going to school (as now I'm home educated), Mum would pack my lunch and put it in my school bag, along with my water bottle in the side pocket. If Mum didn't do that and I did it—it wouldn't matter how many times Mum would try to teach me otherwise— I would still forget my lunch and my water bottle would end up inside my bag and all over everything else. Mum was happy to do this part of our morning routine as I think it helped her sanity. As I get older I'm sure I will become better with such things, but honestly—I watch Mum do the same things for my Dad and he has a saying that "if his b . . . . weren't in a bag, he'd forget them too!". That's a figure of speech, maybe a little inappropriate, that my Dad taught me—I will cover such things with my Dad later!

When I would get home from school, Mum would sort out my bag— this was also for her sanity! Otherwise she would not know what was going on if there were any notes and she could not stand it if my bag was so messy! It wasn't messy to me! If I was bringing something real important home, like the new book club magazine—I wouldn't even put it in my bag; I would hold onto it and make sure I gave it to Mum. In my opinion, that was the only real important note.

Even with my fairly regular type of morning routine, most mornings I will still have Mum nagging me to be quicker, 'hurry up' 'what part of fast, don't I understand?', 'we don't have much time left', 'have you finished your breakfast?' and sometimes she would threaten to turn off the TV! As I said, I get there, just nowhere near as quickly as my Mum and maybe other people.

About school, why am I now being home educated? It had taken until the end of Semester One of Grade 5 for my life at school to get to the point of exploding. Other years have certainly had their moments with lots of intervention from Mum but this year apparently Mum wasn't allowed to intervene. My 'older style' teacher felt that I needed to do it all on my own because I was now 10 years of age and that it was simply just me being non-compliant or having inappropriate or bad behaviour. A classroom situation or group situation does not work for me and if my teacher is not understanding of this, I do have bad or inappropriate behaviour. If the teacher proceeded to yell at me or raise their voice, my behaviour would escalate. In the first school I attended, they would prefer to send me outside to sit and think about what I had done. Most of the time I didn't know what I had done and while sitting outside I certainly wasn't learning anything.

Mum and Dad liaised with my last school on several occasions and also made sure that my unofficial diagnosis was now made official. None of it seemed to help. It did not matter what Mum requested even with the support of CAMHS, the school would not change their mindset or attitude on any of it but insisted they were doing what was best for me! The most difficult part was having to say goodbye to my friends, but I still keep in touch with them and have outside activities like karate that help in this area.

One of the most traumatic times for me at school was sports days, fitness in general and working together in a group. Due to the expectations of school, I was made to endure these activities even though they would cause me many more problems. It is one of the major aspects of mainstream schooling I do not miss. Another aspect was music—even though I play the piano and love it—at school I had to play a brass instrument. I was really looking forward to playing the trumpet but I wasn't long into my lessons when my mouth began to hurt. We did not realise I would have sensory issues with it and again, my teacher was not understanding.

Home schooling is not a viable option for everyone due to things like family commitments, both parents having to work and families with other siblings. Thankfully for us, so far (it is only early days) having to leave the mainstream schooling system has been what Mum calls 'a blessing in disguise'. It really suits our lifestyle and Mum makes almost everything we do into a school excursion or learning experience. Mum is also aware that if I fall behind or don't learn the required work, that she will be the ultimate one to blame and at this stage she 'puts on a brave face' and does her best to cope with this. I mean we have to blame Mum, she gave birth to me—so it must be her fault that I have aspergers! Although this is a joke, just because Mum is now my teacher, it doesn't mean that I am now an angel of a student! Mum reckons not all parents could cope with teaching a child with aspergers due to my attitude and constant need of having to be kept on track. There are days when I'm sure Mum would rather just send me back to a mainstream school and I guess it's always an option. One that at this point in time, I really don't want to pursue.

Home Schooling is like another world, there is so much information, support and guidance out there, that we don't have enough hours in a day to fit it all in. Mum is asked questions about it all of the time, so between my aspergers and home educating we feel a bit under pressure at times from others expectations. That's when we put our positive affirmations in to place to overcome the negative and draining connotations.

Simple Points to remember from this Chapter:
- Clothes routine
- Morning Routine—Mum's jobs and my jobs
- Personal Hygiene—teeth, hair and showers!
- My school bag
- Mainstream schooling and Home Educating.

'General Grievous' from Star Wars built in Lego by Harrison

CHAPTER 2

PLANNING FOR MY OWN SHED

I wondered if you'd guessed I collect things and like to keep them—forever! And I also like to keep the box they came in,—for everything—, forever!

Mum tells people I already need my own shed—I'd be happy with that. Mum made a compromise with me to help with keeping all of my boxes. With the small ones that have plastic on the front for something like a Starwars figure—she will take the plastic part off and she is allowed to place that in the recycle bin. But the other part, usually the back with the details on it—I get to keep. They go into a draw—and although I don't usually get them out very much—you never know, I may!

With such things like large lego boxes, Mum again cuts off the side that I want to keep usually with the most details on it. Then she is also allowed to place the other bits into the recycle bin. Mum says it's good to recycle too, so we are both happy!

Mum has large plastic containers in the shed from basically when I was born to now. She puts all of my drawings and work in them. At times she has tried to go through these with me to down size, but it hasn't been very successful. The containers are easy to store and I don't see the problem with it. I have a tray or draw in the house and when it gets full, Mum transfers it to the large plastic container—and yes, I would notice if she tried to throw them out!

I still have all of my Thomas the tank engine stuff! It is also in a large plastic container and I even get to use it if a younger friend comes over—I am always happy to get it out and play with it, with them.

Next was my Ninja Turtles stuff and Mum now has that packed up in few plastic containers in the shed. Mum is hoping we can give it away to someone special who will look after it like me—one day. As that is how I got a lot of my toys and special things—so when I pass it on, and if I pass it on—it is very important that it goes to someone who is going to appreciate it like me and look after it? Mum has made the mistake in the past where she has convinced me to give some of my stuff to some of my friends who need it more than me—and later I have witnessed them not looking after it—and that really affects me!

From there I have moved on to Lego, particularly Starwars stuff. I'm in the Lego club and would like to own my own Lego factory one day! Mum tried to move me on from Lego by introducing me to Warhammer—where you build little miniatures and paint them. You can then play a strategy board game with them. This worked as I love it, but I also want to own my own Warhammer shop one day too. Both Lego and Warhammer are very expensive hobbies, so Mum says!

I would be happy to buy some Warhammer, Lego or electronic games every day. The problem is, I'm too young to have a job and Mum worries about me even getting a job if I don't learn a few skills in the meantime—and 'money doesn't grow on trees', I know that figure of speech!

Most Mum's are pretty soft (except perhaps mine!) and my Nanny was pretty soft—if I walked around the shop with the item in my hand the whole time, they would sometimes give in to me or give me a few dollars to go towards it. Nanny has sadly passed away, but I do have some other lovely friends who do the same. The problem with getting a few dollars to go towards it is—I want it NOW! For me, if I don't buy it NOW—someone else might buy it and I will miss out! And even if there are quite a few on the shelf, to me they could all go before I have the money saved up. And if there is only one there, it's like the end of the world—I mean, it's the last one!!! Mum and I have come up with a compromise for this type of situation too and I hope it may work for you.

If it's not too expensive, Mum will buy it and I am not allowed to open it until I have paid her back. Mum is strong though—as I will carry it around with me unopened—and everyone else feels sorry for me except my Mum. In fact some people have even told Mum she's being mean, but that doesn't stop her from making me pay her back first! I would even sleep with it unopened and that's not very comfortable!

The better option for Mum particularly is the lay-by system! As I am older now, I am allowed to have two lay-bys going at one time. But no more than two! Initially when Mum explained it to me and we placed my Lego on lay-by—it was very traumatic for me to watch the shop assistant wrap it in black plastic and put it away. It took a lot of convincing that I would be getting it back at the end of paying off my lay-by. This has now helped me with my maths and Mum is big on budgeting, so she believes it helps with that too.

How do I pay for them? Remember that lovely friend I mentioned, I help her with her grocery shopping and she gives me sometimes up to $5.00, to Mum's disapproval! I also do a few chores to earn pocket money. Mum reckons in her and Dad's day they had lots of chores to do and they didn't' get pocket money—so I am very lucky. Now, I don't believe I'm very lucky at all when one of my chores is cleaning up the doggy doo! And in winter it really sucks! In fact for a time I made up excuses and didn't do it, so I didn't' earn any pocket money—and I really wanted to buy some cool things. Mum reckons I whinge excessively when it comes time to do my chores, but I still do them whinging and all!

I also have a phobia towards bees. I've never been stung by one and never want to be, but I am very scared of them. For some reason I imagine that if there is a bee flying past me it is going to definitely make a 'bee-line' for me and sting me! This also drives Mum insane when she has a lovely rose garden and loves bees. I take my dog, Jessie, out with me when I clean up her doggy doo hoping for her protection—but when she annoys the bees I end up running inside screaming! Jessie used to be allergic to bees and now she eats them—this doesn't help my phobia! The doggy doo eventually gets done and I also take the bins in and out once a week. I also bring the neighbour's bins in if he is not home—Mum says even little things count when helping other people.

I totally believe that I earn my pocket money to go on my lay-bys!

I also trade games for my electronic games. This is a bit tricky, as I have to be really sure that what I'm trading in is a game or games that I'm totally finished with or bored with—and that what I'm getting in return is going to be better! There have been a few occasions where a 'meltdown' has arisen due to my trading! The shop assistants who work there know me quite well as I'm always asking them questions about how much it is to trade this one and that one in. I also have to make sure I take really good care of them, so that I can maybe trade them in one day in the future. I've tried trading some of my Dad's games in but they have scratches on them!

The lay-by system and trading games is a great compromise for Mum and I, and it works for us and will also assist me in my future.

With my hording stuff, I have been known to sell some stuff in one of Mum's garage sales that we may have every few years! And because Mum is big on giving to others, we call this blessing others, especially those who are less fortunate than us—I have been known to do this also! I have given some of my stuff to charities who then share them out to some children who may not have any toys. (That is hard for me to imagine and I feel really sad for them).

Another 'funny' worth a mention is my need to take something with me when we go out, even if it's just down the street! Mum needs to give me what she calls 'warning orders' anyway and she also has to take into account that I NEED to take something with me. This is usually not a drama until I haven't planned it and can't find it when it's time to go! So, the better option would be to have things ready the night before (Mum does this with long day trips or overnighters). But for short trips, when I get the first 15 minute warning order—I really need to be getting my things ready for what I want to take with me! As if I leave it to the last 5 minute warning order—it can be disastrous! I take things like, books to draw in, books to read or my Starwars or Halo figurines. These all end up in Mum's handbag eventually, which is another issue—but so far we both can live with it! Remember it's always best to make sure your Mum has a big handbag with room enough for your important stuff!

Just a word on timers. With my warning orders, we have a timer from one of Sue Larkey's workshops and it works a treat, if Mum remembers to put it on. It helps us both know how much time we have left to do something or to get something ready. When I can see how much longer I have left, it makes it much easier—although most times I still believe I haven't had enough time. (So I still might 'crack it', but Mum just ignores this!)

Simple Points to remember from this Chapter:
- Boxes and recycling
- Plastic containers and storage ideas
- Expensive Hobbies

- Lay-by system and pocket money
- Warning Orders
- The need to take things out
- Use of a visual timer

Harrison's 10th Birthday party with ice-cream cake

CHAPTER 3

NOT EATING WHAT EVERYONE ELSE EATS, STILL ENTITLES YOU TO DESSERT!

We have covered breakfast but we haven't covered the other meals of the day or snacks! Mum has had so much fun with this one! Of course when Mum was a child she had to sit at the table and eat everything before she went to bed and if she never ate her main meal—there is no way she would get dessert! So then she had a son like me! If I don't like something, there is no point forcing me to eat it as sadly I end up throwing it up or feeling really sick. So, sitting there all night is not going to help. And yes, I will go without dessert if I have too and if I really want dessert, then I may attempt it at the cost of throwing up!

Nanny (who made my Mum sit at the table) would say," just give him what he wants, if he only wants a cheese sandwich for dinner, let him have it!" I loved my Nanny for many reasons and this was one of them! She got it! Then when we'd go out for tea, Mum would have to take a cheese sandwich out for me—as it was a waste of money buying me a children's meal or any meal. And some people would have a go at Mum—but Mum and I now realise that those people have a go at you either way! Mum had to get used to getting strange looks from other people while Dad and her had a luxurious tea and I sat there with my cheese sandwich! And we were happy, it worked.

At school, lunch time and recess were difficult as I am a very slow eater. Thankfully Mum is too, so she understood. She would tell the teacher that I was allowed to eat half of my sandwich for recess and then the other half for lunch. This way, I then got some play time and I also got to eat my sandwich. <u>Play time was extremely important.</u>

Mum would get embarrassed when we were eating with other children and they would comment on "How come Harrison gets dessert when he didn't finish his meal?" Like they thought it was soooo unfair. Would they prefer me to just throw up on them?! Mum would explain that it's a sensory/texture thing and I was still entitled to my dessert! They never believed her, but I have dessert every night—even if it is just a fredo frog! Mum's a real 'sweet tooth' so she gets that!

I won't even drink 'bits' in fruit juice! And when we are out I have special orders for most places. When we would go to MacDonald's I would have to have my cheeseburger without pickles or onions! 'Wendy's' hotdogs are the only hotdogs I eat and without butter, only sauce. And I won't eat a meat pie unless it is a mince meat pie! Or at another place I won't have ice-cream in my milkshake. Some shop assistants have a real bad attitude about it too; they think I'm just trying to be difficult.

Like Mum says, life is too short to get bent out of shape (a figure of speech!) over the small issues such as food. There are many more important things in life to worry about. And you have to bounce off other people's views and attitudes. I'm still healthy and although Mum reckons I could actually tone up a bit more—I don't fall ill very often and when I do, I usually get better quickly. I'm still growing and get to enjoy things like karate where I need energy. I haven't suffered too much for eating mostly cheese sandwiches and fredo frogs!

Simple Points to remember from this Chapter:

- Food—texture and meals
- Eating Out
- Being a slow eater.

Harrison near the Sydney Opera House before doing
the Sydney Harbour Bridge Climb

CHAPTER 4

RULES OF ENGAGEMENT

ood Manners and Sharing. You know how aspergers is for life—well, not that Mum knew she had a son with aspergers when I was first born, but she was very aware that I would be an only child due to her women's history. Mum was aware of family, friends and even people she didn't know having a go at her about spoiling an only child and how one child doesn't learn how to share properly and they don't get enough interaction with other children. This made Mum furious and she was going to do everything in her power to counteract what they would say or imply—and as such it has helped with my aspergers!

Some of the things Mum put in place from when I was basically born became rules to me and hence have helped me with my aspergers. One of the simple rules are good manners of 'please' and 'thank you'. Also Mum would ask me to look at people when I talked to them as apparently that was also good manners. I would find this difficult, and

Mum would say that it would hurt their feelings if I didn't look at them when I spoke. Over time it has become a rule that I do my best to follow in my daily routine. Mum still keeps an eye on this and will soon correct me if I do forget.

Smiling is something I don't do much unless I'm having a big belly laugh or doing something most probably inappropriate! Mum now says to people who think I'm not happy when I actually am—that's Harrison's smile! Sometimes you wish they'd just lay-off and mind their own business.

It's like washing your hands after the toilet, again Mum would say germs would get under my fingernails, one's I couldn't see and they'd make me sick! Now, there may be some truth to that—but it really was one of those 'figures of speech' type things that worked for Mum, until I was old enough to work out the truth! It has helped me to continue to wash my hands though, and she still asks or checks!

Mum would invite other families around with young children of around my age and organise game days or craft days. They were usually around Easter and Christmas as this was also a time of giving. Everyone seemed to really enjoy them and it was only usually me who would find them difficult. For one, I had to share my Mum with other kids and they were asking her how to do things—and I had to wait! Then there was the noise factor, the screaming kids and the chaos of children wanting to go into my room. After a while, I would usually have a 'meltdown'. We soon learnt that after a while, it would be best for me to go and have some quiet time on my own—and then re-join the group. My room was out of bounds and the play room had enough toys in there for everyone. With these days, I had no option but to learn how to share and accept working with people in a group, but it helped to always have Mum there to intervene. I would also help Mum to give out the gifts or Easter eggs at the end—and no one went home without some sort of gift or item they had usually made. These days, although a challenge at times, were and still are proactive in my journey. I usually know now if someone or something is getting to me, and I just let Mum know I'm going to my room for some time out and she understands.

Mum would also organise 'play dates' and to this day we still have them. In fact, I can be totally booked out with social dates! I've learnt that only one friend over at a time works best—as even then we still have our moments. I usually still need some quite time for myself. Mum is good at mediating when things get a bit heated and Mum explains to my friends the reason why I might be upset about something. My friends are very understanding and cope well with my 'funnies'. They even cope with if I have an accident overnight, which really helps as I get so embarrassed about it.

Mum and I have a routine with this situation and I can even sleep over friend's houses now—as I used to get too worried about having an accident there. I wear dry nights and my friends don't tease me about that. I also have a terry cotton draw sheet that fits over the bottom sheet. I can then comfortably sleep somewhere without worrying about having an accident. The next morning, I then roll the draw sheet up with my pj's and dry night (which I place in a small plastic bag) and then take them home to be washed. This all fits in my bag without anyone having to know. When I get dressed in or out of my pjs I can also do this in privacy without anyone knowing I have dry nights on. I usually take a torch with me too.

At home in the mornings, I am now old enough that if I have an accident I can place the draw sheet and my pjs into the washing machine. Mum has two draw sheets so that one can be drying and the other one can be used that night if needed. If we go away on holidays, we also use this routine and Mum takes both drawsheets.

Pets. Having a pet is a known factor in helping all children with or without special needs. Again, it can depend on lifestyle to what type of pet would suit your family and individual needs. I got to choose Jessie, our dog, when she was a puppy and I was 4 years of age. Jessie has then grown up with me and she is allowed to sleep on my bed, which helps with my anxiety. Jessie is great because she is never angry or upset with me, no matter how I'm traveling. Jessie always has a doggie smile for me and is always happy to have a cuddle or a play. Jessie is very important to me, so this can add to another type of anxiety; for example, when she is outside of our house—I panic that she may be hit by a car. When we go away, I'm always so looking forward to being reunited with Jess. She loves me for who I am all of the time. Jessie is an easy pet to look after and thankfully she only eats dry food—so this helps with me cleaning up her doggy doo!

My Dad was given an orphaned baby emu, named Charlie 7. When we stay with Dad, we babysit Charlie at times. Charlie is similar to Jessie but does more poops! Charlie is also a bit like me, she doesn't particularly like you to invade her personal space, but she will come up and snuggle in when she is sleepy. I think Charlie has anxiety too, because if she cannot see us she cries out in despair. I always feel very calm around pets.

One rule I'm still working on, is talking about my interest/hobby. As for me, that is normal and I don't see the point in talking about other topics and although I try to with my friends, I get bored quickly. And with my interest I don't understand why everyone else doesn't get it like me—like why wouldn't they?! It's soooo interesting and easy to talk about, like I could forever.

To help me to understand sharing and thinking of others, we sponsor some children. Mum and Dad already sponsored a girl from Africa and then one day I went through the 'walk through' tent for Compassion. Mum knew that by the end of it I would want to sponsor a child, so I got to choose who we should sponsor. We sponsor a boy my age in another part of Africa. It would be even more difficult to talk to him, but I get to write to him and that's hard enough—because they really don't have anything like we have. I still don't really understand it, but I do know that he has nothing much compared to me and we are really blessed here in Australia.

Another rule I've had to learn is how to say thank you for a gift even if I don't want it or like it. Mum learned very quickly that I say it how it is, so she helped me to learn this rule and I was then allowed to discuss the gift or how it felt later with her, when we were on our own. Discussing things later with Mum is always good, because I need to tell someone about some of the things that really grose me out—especially as I'm not allowed to say them then and there! And I can trust Mum. Sometimes after school Mum could tell when she picked me up that I was upset, so we would go out and have a hot chocolate and a chat. I could then explain to her everything that happened. If we had been out with other people and I was unlucky enough to be sitting next to someone who was eating with their mouth open and maybe spitting food out while they were talking—it would grose me out so much that I would have to chat to Mum about it later. I would really want to say something right there and then, but instead now I move away if I can, and then I talk to Mum about it later.

I also had to learn that what I said would or could hurt others feelings. If someone's breath smelt I was quite happy to tell them because it was the truth and how could they not notice it? I got into trouble a few times at school for saying things like this or while out with Mum and Mum would have to step in and apologise—and I really didn't understand why she was apologising. I mean, it was the truth. As I have become older, I have learnt to be able to walk away. If I want to blurt something obvious out, I try to walk away first. I also do this if someone is annoying me, too noisy or too close to me. Deep breathing and walking away can help the situation.

Mum tries to stay calm all of the time but sometimes she will lose it at me. Yelling at me or even raising your voice is absolutely terrible for me, not just from Mum but from anyone. I hate to be yelled at in any way. I also do not like to be hit in any way and if I am hit, it hurts me physically really bad. This is a tricky one, because if a person hits me or yells at me—even if it's by accident—I become very angry, a bit like the hulk—although that's my Dad! So a rule I'm not so good at and still learning is to stay calm, deep breathe and maybe to walk away.

Figures of Speech. As you can tell from my previous chapters, Mum enjoyed using 'figures of speech' to her advantage when I was little. Because I take things literally, she could get away with saying things that would put fear in me to do the right thing. This turned out to be good in some ways and it also did help me to learn about 'figures of speech' as I got older. Early on when someone would say something to me and Mum could pick up that I took it literally—she would quickly add that it was a figure of speech. Mum taught me early on that if something was a figure of speech, it had a different meaning and wasn't always what I thought they had really said. Now, as I continue to grow up, I will actually ask a person if that was a figure of speech, if they leave me wondering with what they have said. By asking them straight out, it quickly clarifies it. For some people they pick these up really quickly, I get there in the end. Another good reason to learn about 'figures of speech' is to help against bullies who will try to set you up!

I have also learnt to ask questions as I go along in life, particularly if it is concerning an activity I may have anxiety about. For example; going down water slides. The Beach House at Glenelg in South Australia is great fun and their water slides are awesome. The great thing about them is that the pool is not deep at the end of the ride. You can also go down in an inflatable raft with one or two other friends. At other waterslide venues I have had to ask the slide security person how deep it is at the end once you hit the water. I then need to work out if I feel confident enough to land in it without too much fuss. When I get it right, it's great—when I don't it's quite disastrous and I then NEVER EVER want to do it again. Asking questions is a vital part of me feeling safe when doing activities, particularly new ones.

Sensory Meltdowns. Mum only learnt recently the difference between a behavioural meltdown and a sensory meltdown. Mum has my behavioural meltdowns worked out—she knows to stay calm and how to deal with me. But Sensory meltdowns, what to do?!!! A recent example is when on our morning walk (where I stay to the side away from the flowers due to bees, oh and I have the fear of bird's pooping on my head) and bang a bug flew into my eye. Mum reckons the whole street would have heard me and I didn't' care and Mum was not helping matters—because she wanted to get the bug out of my eye. There was no way I was going to let her touch me and I was already screaming and in a fit. She said we could go to the Doctors to have it removed and I screamed louder.

Then she wacked me across the ears as to try and stop my frenzy— and that really hurt! She yelled at me and that made it worse! She did actually get a tissue out and dabbed my eye with it for the bug to cling hold of—and that really hurt! We quickly walked back home and Mum tried to get me to rinse out my eyes—as if that was going to happen! I did try and finally I calmed down. Mum says in a medical type situation, she can't help me if I don't try to help myself—and to help myself I really need to stay calm. But how do you do that when it feels like you are being attacked and are in so much pain? I know I'm meant to stay calm! Staying calm and learning how to stay calm is one of the most important rules I need to learn for my everyday living, but it's not easy.

Affirmations. These help me with learning positive thinking and retraining my brain to be positive. Sometimes Mum can't believe how negative I am in an instant. The negative words just flow out and it horrifies Mum who believes they are harmful. Mum goes to great lengths to keep me positive and to learn how to use positive language. Positive affirmations are one way, reading positive books together is another and having our strong faith, with prayer time is another. There are plenty of books around on positive thinking and recently we went to a seminar held by Doctor Caroline Leaf who taught us how to grow good healthy thoughts (trees) in our brain and not thorns! So instead of it being the 'end of the world' or if something goes wrong and I NEVER want to try it again, Mum makes sure I get a full does of positive affirmations right then and there—she even makes me repeat them after her. Now, when I'm around negative people, I don't like it and that helps me to try and remember that I don't want to be like that either.

I also see a wonderful counsellor at Child and Adolescent Mental Health Services, CAMHS. I have been doing this since I was sent there with 'anger management issues' in kindy. This is my second counsellor from CAMHS and both of them have been wonderful. I go there and get to talk about all sorts of things and even whinge about my Mum if I want too! These sessions also help me learn new things and strategies for my daily journey.

Simple Points to remember from this Chapter:
- Good Manners
- Sharing and giving
- Play Dates and Sleepovers
- Talking it out
- Figures of Speech
- Asking Questions
- Anger Management
- Sensory Meltdowns
- The importance of affirmations

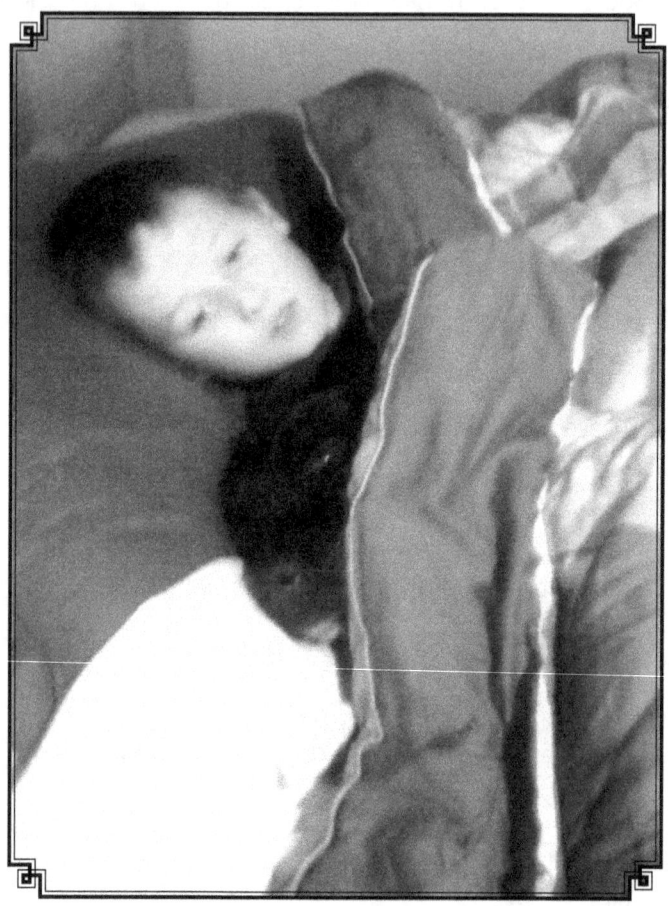

Harrison and Jessie ready for bed

CHAPTER 5
SCARED—WHO ME?

This Chapter is really important and Mum nearly left it out! Anxiety is one of those things that is always with me no matter what I do to overcome it! Mum reckons I'm scared of my own shadow at times—and I don't find this very funny at all!

Thankfully I know that I'm not the only person scared of the dark and I even have a friend who is in her seventies and she is still scared of the dark and she doesn't have aspergers. So how do we put things in place to have victory over our anxiety?

Bed time. Mum still has a job to get me out of her bed, especially as Dad works away! I have my own double bed that I share with Jessie, my dog. I can leave the light on all night and Jessie sleeps on my bed with me and yet I am still scared. I would rather be in with Mum even though Jessie has more chance of protecting me than Mum! When I sleep in Mum's bed (and Mum bought a king size bed as she was annoyed with having my company nearly every night!), Jessie still sleeps on my bed and she really thinks it is totally her bed. Then when I do sleep with her, she growls at me if I push her out of the way—how rude!

I also try to get Mum and Dad to sleep in the same room as me but in another bed—so we also have another double bed in our house— due to my sleeping habits! My bed or Jessie's bed is on one side of the room and then there is a cupboard in the middle and a double bed on the other side—so there is no door in-between. This helps a little bit, but Mum and Dad still prefer their own bedroom, with a door and larger bed. Mum even tries to pay me a dollar if I sleep in my own bed all by myself and allow her and Dad to sleep in their own room—this sometimes works because it's only for a few nights when Dad is home and I can usually get through that—with the light on and Jessie on my bed with me. Mum also knows she won't go broke because it's only for a few nights.

I don't like dark places and going into a room that looks dark by myself or being first to enter. So going to public toilets was always a problem and I would go into the ladies with Mum—much too many peoples disbelief. I stopped when there would be girls in there my age and it made me feel really embarrassed. But I am super quick in public toilets and Mum waits not too far outside the door for me.

Crossing the road or being around cars in a car park affects me. If there is a lot of traffic I will still hold my Mum's hand and I don't care what others think, because I feel safe. It's only for a short time while I cross the road, so I will put up with anyone's comments. They usually just look but don't say anything. In busy car parks I stay close to Mum and she says I nearly trip her over at times, but I feel safe.

I also become scared of certain things like characters from movies—and this can be really damaging. It consumes my mind and makes life very difficult. I have to constantly work on overcoming my fear of this type and I always discuss it with my Counsellor thoroughly. We do our best to come up with new strategies to overcome it. One example is a trip we did to Universal Studios. I only saw a particular character once, whose name cannot be mentioned, from a distance and although Mum wouldn't let me go into the "House of Horrors", my cousins told me all about it. I had nightmares for months and months. Even friends just talking about a scary movie can affect me because I take it literally. I don't even have to have seen the movie but what they tell me can leave me with a lasting impression. Of course I don't want to tell them that what they are talking about is scaring me. Mum and I then have to work through it later. Talking it out or turning it into something funny in my mind when it is mentioned.

Anxiety is a difficult one, sometimes I would rather feel embarrassed and deal with it my own way than be totally scared and upset. So, sleeping in with Mum or with the light on all night—or holding Mum's hand crossing the road or nearly landing on her when I am scared of cars or bees—is all part of me coping with my anxiety within my surroundings. All of the affirmations, prayers and positive thinking in the world cannot help me at times. It is one of those things I am still learning to deal with in life.

Simple Points to remember from this Chapter:
- Anxiety
- Nightmares and darkness
- Movie characters

Harrison and his Dad, putting his new bike together.

CHAPTER 6

"THE APPLE DOESN'T' FALL FAR FROM THE TREE"

My Dad! Now just between you and I, Mum and I reckon Dad has aspergers—of course it's undiagnosed and will never be diagnosed—but we have a chuckle about it. It has also helped Mum to work strategies out with me. Mum is the 'No Fun Police' and Dad is lots of fun when he's not angry! That's when he has the capacity to turn into the Incredible Hulk and that's what Mum is trying to teach me not to do!

Luckily Dad works away a lot and now that I'm finally used to it, Mum reckons it's just as well because Dad sort of teaches me some things that are a bit inappropriate—but what I really love! Dad is also into thinking that farting is fun—so he will do it in a lift full of people and that's also how he wakes me up in the morning! Very inappropriate but very funny!

Mum would say to him "You are going to get Harrison into trouble at school—as he copies you!" Well part of it was copying I guess, and the other part is that Dad and I are very much alike. We both think that farting, burping and doing some silly things are very funny! Mum says there is a time and a place and tries to get Dad and I to just do it when we are together away from other people! Mum says to me, "would you leave that for when you are with your Dad, it's not appropriate now or here!"

Dad is also very good at telling people the truth and telling it as it is—and for him as an adult, he can mostly get away with it in his job. But for me, it really has gotten me in to a lot of trouble at school and sometimes out in public places. If Dad is home when I have friends over, they have to cope with the both of us being what Mum calls, 'Grose"!

A trait of aspergers can be wanting to be perfect and never wanting to fail. Mum insists I remain positive and always have a go and that it's not the end of the world. I don't agree with her that often but I do know that it is another underwritten rule—to stay positive and to train your brain to be positive. Dad does airbrushing and he is really good at it—but if Mum doesn't take the picture away from him in time when it's finished—he will paint over it because he believes it is not good enough, although everyone else loves it! I can be a little bit like this with my Warhammer! And if I get maths questions wrong, Mum has a hard time keeping me positive. There is a saying something like 'Failure is success turned inside out". And we learn from our mistakes, they are not to be a negative part of our life. We can turn it into a positive although we may not think so at the time.

My Dad is also more open to me watching things that are 'M' rated, although since I've had the diagnosis—he has joined Mum in force a bit more on this. Mum tries real hard to put boundaries in place with electronic games and what I watch on TV. I have to read the books of "Harry Potter" and "The Lord of the Rings" before I watch them! But Dad, he will let me watch "Mr Creaso" on "Monty Python" and then we have fun reciting it afterwards. And Dad and I enjoy playing "Halo" on the xbox much to Mum's disgust.

Mum says Dad's desensitized and that I am too literal for such things—that's why she is happy Dad works away for now! In the early days of Dad working away I would give Mum a really hard time because I don't like change and I couldn't understand why Dad had to go away. It took a few years of learning strategies to put in place and now we cope when Dad is away and enjoy when he is home. I get to talk to him every night on the phone.

I still wish that my Dad was home every night but I do believe it might send Mum a bit crazy with what we both get up too. I think Mum can only cope with us both in small doses and well, she has to cope with me every day and that can be hard work—so she reckons. Mum believes I'm worth every bit of hard work though. Dad and Mum both love me very much and it is wonderful to have their constant love and support when at times I feel so different from everyone else and like I don't fit in.

Simple Points to remember from this Chapter:
- Inappropriate Behaviour
- Wanting to be perfect
- Parents who live away from you

Aspergers can be a wonderful journey and although we still have our ups and downs, or our more challenging days—because we are still learning up until the day we pass on—we know that we can have fun along the way and make our special journey one worth traveling along.

Between Mum, Dad and I, we have learned to make the most of aspergers and Mum particularly says it's a positive 'special need'. She believes that great things can happen with me and my aspergers in my future—and I know that the same is true for you. Like me, we just have to stay positive and to remember to always believe in ourselves. I intend to do just that and hope that along the way I can also help other people with and without aspergers, because aspergers can be fun!

References and Resources:

Making it a success with Sue Larkey—www.suelarkey.com

Controlling toxic thoughts and emotions—Dr Caroline Leaf, www.drleaf.com

Joyce Meyer Ministries—www.joycemeyer.org

Compassion (Sponsor a child)—www.compassion.com

The complete guide to Asperger's Syndrome by Tony Attwood—www.tonyattwood.com.au

My Aspergers Child, by Mark Hutton—www.myaspergerschild.com

CAMHS—Child and Adolescent Mental Health Services, South Australia

Author: Harrison Allam sdallam@bigpond.com